Also by Toni Thomas:

Chosen
Fast as Lightening
Walking on Water
Blue Halo
Ace Raider of the Unfathomable Universe
You'll be Fast as Lightning Coveting my Painted Tail
Hotsy Totsy Ballroom
Love Adrift in the City of Stars
In the Pink Arms of the City
In the Kingdom of Longing
The Things We Don't Know
In the Boarding House for Unclaimed Girls
They Became Wing Perfect and Flew
Unburdened Kisses
Bandits Come and Remove Her Body in the Night
There is This
Here
The Smooth White Vanishing
Perishing in the Rain
A Different Measure of Moonlight
The Secret Language of River
Inside Her a River of Snow was Traveling
The Arbiter of Her Own Flame
A Bride of Amazement

Paradise on a Shoestring

First published in 2025 by Annalese Press
134 Towngate
Netherthong
Holmfirth
West Yorkshire HD9 3XZ
England

Copyright © 2003 Toni Thomas

*All characters and situations appearing
in these pages are creatures of the imagination and in the
service of poetry.
Any resemblance to real persons
living or dead, is purely coincidental.*

All rights reserved. No part of this publication may be reproduced, stored, or transmitted in any form, or by any means electronic, mechanical or photo-copying, recording or otherwise, without the express written permission of the publisher.

Cover design and layout by Peter Wadsworth
Decoration: The Excursion of Nausicaa,
Ethel Walker, 1920

British Library Cataloguing-in-Publication Data
A catalogue record for this book is available on request from the British Library.

ISBN 978-1-0685744-1-2

Acknowledgments

With appreciation to the following presses for selecting these poems, or a version for publication -

"Easy Hips" Nominated for a Pushcart Prize
Big Muddy: A Journal of the Mississippi River Valley

"Crows" Third Place, The Ann Stanford Poetry Prize 2006
Southern California Poetry Anthology

"Pink Flamingos" appeared in *Margie,*
The American Journal of Poetry

"In the Bowl of Persimmons" appeared in *Alimentum*

Contents

Prologue
    What If   1

Part One: Keeper of the Slumped Down Roses
Crows	5
Arrested Day	7
Axioms of Sin	8
Keeper of the Slumped Down Roses	10
Floating	11
Miracle	12
My Mother tells Me	13
Tyrant	16
Flight 325 to San Francisco	18
The Time Before This One	19

Part Two: Pink Flamingos
Winifred's House	23
Swimming at Jones Beach	25
Spike Heels	28
My Father's Hands	30
Pink Flamingos	32
Snow Fall	33
Levity	35
Family Portrait	37
Delivery	39
Fire Escapes	41

Part Three: Lemons

Lemons	45
Purveyor of Paradise	46
Deliberate Morning	47
Legacy	48
Ironing	48
Prosperity	51
Filial Summer	52
Consummation	53

Part Four: Easy Hips

Easy Hips	57
Missionary	58
Landscape	59
Northwest Courtship	60
Precision	61
Sister	63
House Wife	64
Weeds	65
White Slips	66
Reckoning	67

Part Five: In the Bowl of Persimmons

Paradise	71
Small Voice	73
Lilacs	75
Come June	77
Repentance	78
Restitution	80
Street Woman	82
God	83
You Collude with the Wind	85
In the Bowl of Persimmons	87
Epilogue	89

*Spring has returned. The Earth is like a
child that knows poems.*
　　　　　　　Rainer Maria Rilke

*Ripe summer's sweetness dripped
in pearls from every tree
and into my opened heart
a little drop ran down.*
　　　　　　　Edith Södergran

*Let me fall if I must fall.
The one I am becoming
will catch me.*
　　　　　　　Baal Shem Tov

Prologue

What if the world drank quinine
and I refused the offer
read a different script, entered it
sat in my room for twenty years
watched the nasturtiums grow thin, die
come back up under the widow's shade tree
what if I wore high heel shoes for the cat
ermine for the spiders
lapis lazuli for the black lab
who refuses to leave the altar of my bed.

What if the moon exploded
the world drank
a cup of shattered pieces
the unanchored blue sky's mauling
your dress a covenant
rim of collapse
I no longer refuse to live in.

Eat me up then
for I have fallen ten degrees
from heaven
my eyes are burning.

Part One

Keeper of the Slumped Down Roses

Crows

There is a pool that lives
in a woman's heart
can speak for her.
Song of black crows, spring rain
purple onion
feet so slow they whisper
to the earth as they move.
This pool holds blue shoes
clear water over rock
is the mountain's ache
the devotion of spruce trees
the wind's slipknots splaying.
January may never come back
with its rusted eye of lament.

My father's hands are black crows
spring rain, purple onion
he sleeps in leaf mulch
the city's rind
stumbles to find the entrance to my bed.

I close my eyes
open a different book
it holds painted eggs, an intricate catwalk
uncut snapshots of the moon.

The mother comes home
can't find me anymore.

His wife says *the world is full of seams*
I will rip them apart
find the eternity inside this bed.
The father sleeps on the fire escape
worries about her hands' madness
the landlord's scalpel
radiator with its leaking head.

The stranger dyes his hair yellow
hopes to marry a girl he can't see
one with stilts and sturdy pay
syncopations that devour the moon
spread no black crows over the table's virtue.

I don white lace
disguise the slew of scars up my arm
the black crows in my bed
extol the nimbleness that lets
a girl jump over flame
again and again and again
live to tell about it.

Arrested Day

How many times has my father tamed me
ravaged the shy sister in my bed
abolished the other you
sent you away—a pale child
with no shoes
no lamp burning.

Patter of feet
poster child with no words
mother who turned a blind eye
on the room's raking
this god with his furrowed brow
would be deliverance.
She knife-ended the tree with
her broken pen.

Prickly scaled
you eat missiles of happiness
can never forget black midnight
the rock throated deliriums
first time
he entered you.

Axioms of Sin

At night you colonize children
spill milk, keys
strident angels
the incorrigible tongue.

There is a room
black walls and loose veins
an orphaned man, only girl child
silence thick as fate
the couch, braided rug
alabaster lamp ferreted away.
You who drove the filial ghosts
from my bed
sank fires below the grate
terrain of coffee stains
smashed window
half-forgotten roses.

Collapsed paradise
you have missing teeth
screw on painted nails
bracelets heavy as time bombs
that will one day detonate
what was skillfully exiled away.

Abandoned foot soldiers
you succor children
grow green platelets

from the earth's loving you
senseless again.
Heir to the good angel
who fought back tireless
beside my bed.

Keeper of the Slumped Down Roses

You live in the yellow corncob
skunk cabbage, blue bowl
mesh of the sloped door
in the litter the possum raises
above the world's scorn.

Are some people made this way
dwarfed
only one good eye to see the world by
as if walking on water
takes more than privilege
honeyed devotion
nimble words?

My sister is too maimed for life
too stalwart, ears pricked
over every field burning.
The keeper of slumped down roses
she salutes deformed kittens
jewelweed, slug colonies
gutters the world forgets
that god still clings to.

Floating

I play table tennis with the day
ease the nature of my tendering
know this ball is worth more than
grand slams, pockmarked deliverance.
The black lab looks on
incredulous at how I lob shots
over both sides of the net
wants to partner me
elevate on hind legs
paddle with his paws.

Sometimes is it easy to lift
our dead weight off the carpet
the concrete of the garage
lift and rise like children
not injurious of the braille
the rain's smacking
but succulent as red winged tulips
April with soft petaled flame?

Large dog rises slowly in thin air.
I look on.
Miracles happen.
The pong and the pings
small ball flying from my hand
floating back over the net.
Anya in paradise.
See how it feels.

Miracle

Jelly fish, pink, translucent
frivolous as a woman's loose hem.
I am afraid you might sting
that the boy who pokes holes
doesn't know the price of erasure

marvel at the distances you have come
the storms, surf's pebbled tongue
way you pant into the damp sand
as if faith, the outgoing tide saves
we live in a benevolence beyond quarrel.

Unlike those of us who can walk away
you are the coral stained savior
body's iridescent breath laid bare
victim to any malicious boot
burdened heart willing to betray you.

I pray for a sneaker wave to come
lift you back into the blue hips
of the sea's swaying.

My Mother Tells Me

that on the day I was born
the pizza crusts she was rolling
drifted out the window
and into the next yard.
It was Lope's yard
and because he was an old man
a wise man
he didn't vex his head over
where they came from
just made the sign of the cross
blessed god, the day
brought out his tomatoes
devoured the whole stack
before their warm breath
could escape

and afterwards my mother often
rolled out her dough with the window open
content to let small miracles spread
brighten a stranger's path
pinched landscape.

My mother tells me
the sun sings in a paper boat
mysterious tongue
and because I am a shy child

poor one
I must learn to listen
carry my voice steady
if I am to outlast the rain.

I have told her that
when I am grown
I will stay here
every day will be pudding
chopped meat
chickens that lay eggs big
as a house.
She laughs
plays her Peggy Lee tape
grabs my arms, circles.

On my twelfth birthday
when Bonita Gonzalez, the fortune teller
read my palm
my mother cried for three days
lit the candles of Mary
said she must weave me a coat
for wintering
I am too delicate
in a metal clad world.

My mother worries about me
nests me in her prayer book.

I am the oldest child
useless dreamer
the one who wanders the yard
while in the kitchen the beans burn.

My mother's hands hold a scorched sun
blue rosary, her dead brother's ashes
my heart which she keeps safe in a jar.
And I tell her I don't ever want to go away.
But she knows I will.

Tyrant

There is a tyrant bird in my throat
it eats men's neckties, church pews
mindless repetition
leaves decibels of loneliness
where wings want to be.

I am the daughter of derision
mount curbs, rake field
search the stranger once thrown from my bed.
He has blue shoes, a serial version of happiness
might pass for my mother but it is not true.
He knows nothing of the wider constituency
of her arms.

You can't escape yourself he says but he's dead wrong
blind to the red hot temptress at his door
the one who apostrophes the moon
runs on platinum, pizza, tangos
walks miles over city bridges
to wear down her heels.

There is a tyrant who lives in my throat
pestilence of locusts
children that run naked in a cold wind
stranger who carves me into blue ice
the half sung deathbed.

But when Sunday arrives
I become meadow, devote myself to

the bleeding of the white sisters, to timothy
the dark heart that lives in the divided tree
the loop trail with its band of clear-cuts
the city's breathless
show god how tireless I can be
obedient as the sun
a welcome mat
modest and nimble.

Flight 325 to San Francisco

It could be on a flight like this
the wing fails, engine flames
in a flash my life turns memory
the farewells at the gate
hug after hug of my boy child
daughter with the clothe doll
no one can peel away
the kisses of the man
I've anchored my life to
all taken away.

It can happen in a flash
the detonation of paradise
or slow as a tumbleweed divorced
from the dirt.
I could find myself embryonic
or mere dust
someone's memory of *mother*
or *lover* or *woman who wrote poems*
memory that may or may not outdistance
the hairnets of time's mentoring.

Then will every homily become
a syllable half anointed
swimming away
with my body's song?

The Time Before This One

Vagrant sister
rope towed to the fender
with your hands bleeding.
He drove that black sedan
as if there was no tomorrow
no price to pay
no bleached blonde who wanted
to be in the front seat
kissing.

Your obituary reads an ice field.
But did he ever really know you
with his pocket watch, airtight refrains
version of paradise that boasts prosperity
married to strychnine?

Was there a time before this one
an easy hour that didn't need to
walk on stilts, the voice's pandemic
your life not measured but durable
scallop edged, lady bugged for luck even
some tire gutted quotient of paradise
threading you home?

Part Two

Pink Flamingoes

Winifred's House

In my German grandmother's house
you could hear the floorboards creak
the hiss of the tea kettle
flap of her cat's tail across the window screen.
I thought her porch rocker, trees
the flutter of finch wings
above her porch feeder
would never migrate.

In my grandmother's house
there were not many rooms
but many objects that whispered back.
An etched silver hairbrush, hat boxes
glass rosary, silky comforter, velvet heels
her starched aprons, German strudel
everyday black orthopedic shoes.
They all had their stories to tell
some glamorous as Berlin in the '30's
others war bound, widowed, emptying.

In my grandmother's house
sea breezes found a place to lull
drifted up Plymouth Street
past Dirigglios Portuguese market
straight into her side door.
She never bolted the house
perfumed her rooms
edge trimmed the grass
let her laundered sheets, dresses
on the back clothesline

gather equal the summer heat
evening's unspoken sorrows.

In my grandmother's house
my brother and I didn't need to name
what we could not understand
picked runner beans, salad tomatoes
played beneath the beech tree
as we lived, let the yard bugs live
afternoons liquid inside
the sun's diligence
my grandmother watching us
as she shucked peas in the shade
me feeling almost holy
in this space she reserved for us.

Swimming at Jones Beach

At the boat basin of Jones Beach
my mother and her girlfriend wore pointy glasses
so dark we couldn't see their eyes.
They rubbed our bodies ghost white with sun block
laid out home decorating magazines, cups of Kool-Aid
shouted *get back in here close* then looked away.
Their shouts were not for the boys
but mainly for me
the only eight-year-old who knew how to float
but couldn't swim.

I liked the sea, its dark water, starfish, secrets
way it lapped sand, preyed on slinky bodies
our blanket, lunch cooler, small boys
in the grasp of its wake.

At noon we'd break open wax paper
eat ham sandwiches, chips, pickle.
I'd hide three crème devil dogs in my towel, smile.
Afterwards the blue octopus tube was inflated
yanked over my head. Now they could take their eyes
off me and I was free to go in up past my waist.

My mother's strapless swimsuit clutched a dark petal
sheened turquoise in the afternoon sun
looked good with her mahogany skin

ex-lifeguard shoulders, muscled legs that made men
turn and stare, convinced she was surely my sister
not my mom.

She sauntered into the surf, a blue tease
with the slow pierce of her hips
till finally she broke through the sea's glass skin
plied rhythmic in and out of the waves
her head smaller and smaller as she drank
the sea's ancient song.

Back then I was certain I could watch
my mother forever from the sand
watch her reach past moorage buoys, pleasure boats
straight out toward the open water
a dot on a blue page
creature who laps up sunfish, children
plays them, rides them
grinds them with her fin.

Sometimes I was afraid she'd disappear
let the sea claim her
but she always came back, helped roll up the blanket
desand our bodies, pack the cooler, beach bags
into her friend's car.

I remember my mother swimming at Jones Beach
the stride of her body across hot sand
the anticipation all summer of clear skies
warm sea, sand castles, ice cream

my mother in her low cut tank top
cotton petal pushers as she rammed the
pink flamingo beach towels back into the car
the promise that someday I'd learn to swim like her
navigate the world's wide ocean with my dorsal fin
strong rhythmic arms threading

that she'd be with me forever
never collapse early morning
on the living room carpet
die young of heart failure.

Spike Heels

When my mother's spike heels offered
to walk miles for me
I was leery of their size
pistol polish and shine
the way they dug into dirt
like some women dig into skin
conquer their men.

She wanted to be my sister
borrowed my orange top
shiny hair clips
snap purse with the patent trim.
We could have been twins
who covet each other's secrets
go from pussy to wildcat
spit mace all over the wall.

It was inevitable she'd move in
with her hips slashing
tear up my room, Monet poster
nail her crimson versions of paradise
dead center above my bed.

My mother dug dirt in my heels
spilt words before I could name them
nailed my life, loves, travel
to the bulge of her black book

all my handmade puppets
benevolent princes
pumpkins turned silken carriage
dangled
then taken away.

My Father's Hands

It would be easy to believe my father drank a lot -
his three jobs, night college, mucked childhood.
Only on Sunday did he sleep in, threaten to stay.
He had calloused hands, hardly any hair
in summer snatched yard beetles
thrust them into his metal coffee can
pool of kerosene.

I was afraid of my father's hands
the no mesh of them, way he swatted flies
slammed a tennis ball so ruthless
nobody could return it over the net
was afraid of his unnamed sorrows
dead mother, adopted away sister, military caps
too many schools, one pair of shoes.

My father has traveled through bone
relies on his few stories to grow old by
has traveled some distance from that
catholic orphanage in the Bronx
but still remembers dragging his drunken father home
from 2am bar stools with his eight-year-old might.
His hands can level a mountain
refuse kisses, beer cans
are a fist in a damned up stream.

I am his only daughter, favorite child
the one for whom he snips sprigs of lilac
places them in a bud vase
the one who avoids certain photograph albums

the family ones where my mother's body, worn face
have been scissored away.
She has left blank space on a sea of pages.
The favorite child who has spent years mired in lovers
countries, angel cake, perfect grades
that say nothing about the rain.

Now my father takes a plane across the country
so we can see each other.
We don't talk about his hands
the newspaper headlines he's memorized
my mother's early death from heart failure
my former marriages
lonely brother moving senseless
past the drugs, jobs, women he can't name.

Pink Flamingos

Every winter when the cold set in
my mother scooped away snow
dug bulbs into the hard earth
rammed the long metal legs of
her neon flamingos into the place
Christmas lights might be.

Come May with the tulips lifting
her web chair appeared
anchored till the rust of
autumn rain claims things
and she buttoned her heart.

Who remembers the peonies
shy throated iris, oriental poppies
she drowned all summer
with green fisted devotion
her blue bowls that cupped Asia
later the black walls
multiplying black walls
she painted late night
high up on the stepladder
her chain lit cigarette version
of paradise burning?

Snow Fall

Harsh November
you haven't yet buried my mother
only the leaves
ahead the prospect of holiday turkey
the salvation army bell, paradise scratching
my mother's dissolution diagnosed as
a false alarm, floating gall stone
nothing to remove her permanently
from the once promise her youth bred.

She will live through Christmas
placate the pain moving up her arm
wear her red beret, tiger eye necklace
call me from New Hampshire
with her bird flecked voice.

On the phone line she hears about
my college term, busted marriage
the man I've just met with poems
inked up and down his arm
small room with a door to a little balcony
my spaniel and I have rented for $210 a month.
She never learns about the messed up peroxide
brass bell yellow crown that ends up
at the top of my hair, how I bury it
under a wool cap for the midnight mass service
the way the snow keeps falling, not in fistfuls

but delicate as inside the glass ball I keep
the simple joy of these pared down days
when god seems to be calling me back
past a well of losses.

For five days and nights the snow keeps falling
the trees, road a glaze of ice
cars buried, people's everyday lives halted
while back in the east your heart quivers.

Mother, I never really got to tell you
how god keeps traveling petals
to my cigarette stained hands
sets up a tray table
fuses my peroxide plagued life
to the limbs of trees.

I've decided not to live without you anymore
live with just the phone call of your sudden collapse
three days into the New Year, 3,000 miles away.
Life isn't fair.
It didn't save you.

Harsh winter
I have known you to press wings
sink my room into a thumbnail of light
turn the flaming dress, shy treatise
into a plague of leaves falling
have known you to handrail my day
into a triumph of holy wind.

Levity

No one wanted to admit she was dead
not once and for all
just restive as in sleep
girl in a photograph
levitation
which my brother says is all about
*magnets raising the body invisibly
above the floor.*

No one entered the plea of *forever*
the finality of the crushed shoes
hot wired breath that incubates
children, disease, heart failure
death with its wings flapping
no place to call home.

Forget the funeral, the closed casket
incinerator, her ashes plastic bagged
later rent out to sea.
She never wanted to marry the dead
stolen nature of the face's bleeding
time with its pointy nails.

After the sermon's seamless
we crept into the parlor.
Maybe the cold cuts saved us
the aluminum tear of the pop cans opening
the insignias of happiness—

pickle, cheese, tomato, club sandwich
we held on our plate.
Beyond us
the window's last tutelage
of lace weeping.

Family Portrait

It was unexpected.
Too early for an obituary
for untethered children
who lug grade sheets, loss
in and out of the door.

Diagnosed with only a gall stone
yet three days into the new year
no man's new found kisses
morning tea cup will save you.
Death pressed under like certain
invisible maelstroms that creep
into the heart's suitcase.

Small burial.
You dressed up as you lived
red proclamation
a host of silver bracelets
waiting to jangle
the casket closed
your ashes sped out to sea.

Farewell we will cry, then dry up.
Farewell our father will cry
hate being alone
within a year marry your lost girlfriend
with the cropped hair.

They will sleep away the memories
she can't stand.

Some things are like this.
A new couple in a new house in a new state.
The sermon of your face, life, family
reduced to a box of photos
heaped on the floor of a garage loft.
No picture of you will ever grace their space.

Delivery

You died when a man and woman's might
couldn't hold you
slipped too soon from December's coat sleeves
the house hammered with early snow
a few days before, the bad omen
five chickens frozen to death in the middle of the night
when the propane heater failed them.
All that week deer coming down into the meadow
to haunt our old apple orchard, bare armed trees.

Still birth. The doctor, county nurse
called mid- morning but never came.
Roads too bad we were told afterwards.
They should have seen the blood all over the floor
my father's frozen hands, voice whimpering
his body turned stiff with whiskey
my mama's braid a sunken rope
on the stained bed sheet.
The weeping, all the weeping after my father
fled out the door with his coat, caked boots
bottle trailing.

We buried her up the far meadow
near the split oak tree
dug a hole under two foot of snow
placed in it her little blued body.
She didn't have any hair
her body wrapped careful in the blanket.

Still birth.
Later, I will dazzle the house
with my paper mache puppet shows
clown routines wed out of old clothes
will eat fire, cake batter
to get you out of my bones
the memory of your blue blue face
flecked in snow
my mother's hands groping
father's weeping
homilies bred of a hard stake.

You are the song yanked from my life's worship
the world before words splinter
harsh sounds set in
might have been my liquid sunset
the knowing one
who rinses river water clear
not just the sky with a hole in it
curve ball that never arrives home.

You are the nebula of dreamers
the quiet word, mulched bed
unclaimed one who congregates
with worms, bones, beetles, seed
over and over relives my past
as a reminder of dark holes, black death
banishment
the uncertainty of rising.

Fire Escapes

The night he came to you
with pried open hands, sunken days
you were eight, too young to know the cost
of a dead mother, catholic orphanage
no bicycle childhood
passed down shoes.

Sometimes heaven spares us
what we cannot bear
turns a blind eye on the room's mauling
wraps us in cellophane.
It will take years for some miner's hand
to excavate the black coal laid in this bed.

Thump. Thump.
The iron in your mother's hand
snipes at paisley, shirt sleeves.
She has sewn her mouth shut
can't find many reasons anymore to be here.
Three days into the New Year
her morning tea cup will shatter
she will fall onto the parquet floor
never get up.

Girl on the other side of the country
how many fire escapes will you crouch on
trying to understand
the way beauty can clutch
so many crushed petals
in its mouth?

Part Three

Lemons

Lemons

This table is too perfect to eat on.
Cottage linen bathed in hyacinth
evenly spaced all the way down.
The soup floating petals of nasturtium
sin's cousin with a wig
supplication while the world waits.

But then beauty has its testimonials to tell
teenage girls with their flash of silver braces
promise, strappy chiffon dresses
that girls on the shabby side of town
can only envy.

Keep quiet then
don't broadcast what envy seeks
the smooth curve, carefully shaved legs.

Hush.
It is late March.
Everything wants to breathe pastel.
Joggers squeeze out of gyms
lap the hemisphere of a golf course.
You get your hair streaked lemon
the color of your life -
no run up your stockings
the dinner table mildly beckoning
the god awful leveling
asphalt trees.

Purveyor of Paradise

you stay up late night
grind glass into my good eye
vandalize faith, panties
the sanctity the earth lends
till happiness is a stolen vow.

Purveyor of paradise
you are a ram in sheep's clothing
cousin of the Judas tree
devour the weak
separate wheat from the chaff
the chaff aching
your hands
no nuptial
of the divining rod god sends.

Deliberate Morning

you hold the clipped voice of wolves
my twin sister swimming in brine
yet safe in her blue nightdress.

Is it easy to float
place only deathless birds of paradise
in our coat?

This morning deliberate
as iced red Dorothy shoes
the neighbor's lawn service
gleam of white teeth
the capable, toned thin
ageless bodies
that pass.

Legacy

How will my daughter manage
when all her fairies flee
the golden egg in her palm
turns caustic as nuclear rain?
What will my son know of an
unrequited world?

It is Sunday, we eat French toast
drown it in maple syrup.
I don't talk to them about my fears
the wobbly nature of the world's want
whether they will ever inherit
paradise in America someday.

My daughter fingers her birthday cards
clips on pink wings.
My son goes back to his Legos.
Just nine years old he has no illusion
the world is only fair play
has ships rigged with flame proof wings
crab like arms, an escape capsule
motor that can crash through the sound barrier
send him hurtling through space
in a metal suit.

It takes hours to stockpile his fleet on the floor.
Seconds for the world to be blown apart
one city
one nation
divisible to the last.

Ironing

It doesn't always happen like this
the moon excavating my bed
your hands finding the plush nuances
buried in skin.
I don't want to find myself pining for
what might have happened in this room.

July snipes days.
You divide furniture, CD's, yard tools
books, kitchenware, toys
roll juice glasses in newspaper
box your grandmother's waffle iron
kebab skewers, the large trussing needle
that sews shut our holiday turkey.

Beetles have started coming up through the floor.
My children try to convince me
they mean good luck in our book of folk tales.
It is late, hot.
They want to sleep in their panties.
I go in, snug up their sheets
wonder at their surface calm, trust
the hard hammers that are about to be heaved
a future of cut up weeks
jostle from house to house
hurried shoes, the misplaced lunchbox.

There's an ancient bird that lives in the heart
is full of sin or fusion
depending on the way you look

eats with a crow's devotion
raven's shattered voice.

I may never cross this bridge
from absence to levity
marry summer to my fallow fields
raise a paper lantern in the midst of snow.

After so many years I begin pressing slips
cotton tops, buried rayon
frazzled play things
search trunks for my laciest panties.
It takes time stretching each one out
the *thump thump thump* of the heavy accurate iron
misting collars, skimpy tops, dresses

smoothing out sheets
pillow cases, cropped pants
my eight-year-olds' checkered vest
daughter's skirt pleats
the tissue slips of lace and flimsy
that wander my soul.

Prosperity

In April the frogs come back
to the pond off Wheeler Lane
red flowering current fuse
their scented fans to the sky
and the corruption of paradise
could feel like a fiction.

In April I slip into my paisley dress
reorder my heart's watchtower
pleasure over the field daisy
meadowlark
fox, coyote
as they prosper the grass.

Filial Summer

You are a flood of forsythia
noisy river
hold no assassin
housing crisis
crazy man who cuts his wife
into pieces, buries the parts.

You are wild rice flecked over
the chapel fled lovers
the confectioner's calligraphy
day laborer's devotion
woman who calls mercy out of
the tongue's sweet grass
the blessed child
for whom all yard swings
are noble.

Consummation

Are there girls with cotton wool in their ears
not enough reasons to go home
people who limp away from their life
burn the parlor with its stained couch
bedroom wedded to knife ends?

Come May floods of lilac burst open
court summer's tanned legs
punctuate the stars with their scent.
I don't ever want to die premature
enter no return on my dance card.

Some say the neighbor two down
was lucky the way she escaped the fire
made her way from sleep to landing
then out the third floor window

how the men in yellow macs saved her
or maybe it was she who saved herself
found a small voice
hand that moves neither
impatient nor devouring
but nascent about her bed.

Part Four

Easy Hips

Easy Hips

It could end like this
a car full of children
your crushed cans littering the road
this man who grinds conceit into my bed
stays up late night fabricating
a blue epistle.

Come nightfall, after the children's
supper, bath, frog game
kisses that want to staple happiness
to a stenciled wall
you breath absence in the parlor
where the couch weeps
rain has rotted the floors.

You counted on my easy hips
blind version of thirst
the ventriloquist's skillset
that never choirs catastrophe
stays glue gunned in place.

September carries debris
the promise of gold leafed autumn
a paradise with less spiny teeth
gulls, an ocean
cottage with a modest slope
children naked, saved
relearning their mother's wild treasons.

Missionary

He wanted perfect
the fine wrought crystal
walls that never bust
women who exercise their
unheard furies away
time with its pointy nails
calibrated.

She swept out his closet
double faced words
knew other men like this
stealthy ones
who eat your trust
heart's desire
poems
leave you trapped
in a small fenced yard
minding their will
children, geranium

men with deaf ears
who devour the dark
their raven's appetite
for porn, whiskey
hot emails
pawing.

Landscape

There are hailstorms that come
pummel the children's sand box
yard toys
eat the girl with the stained dress
reduce things to an ice field
swollen wishes without a home.

Strident sister in your pink negligee
I have seen you polish spoons
scrub lawn, carpet
whip up mocha gateau.

Boot camp, training ground
ulcer that grows big as a man's fist
pocket flashlight to see the world by
my blue notebooks
sullen moon in the bed
husband who eats derision
makes other women's ruby lips
his prey.

Northwest Courtship

It is February
the month people fall out of windows
rope swings rust
clothes get devoured by rain
with nobody in them.

You decide to warm with paper valentines
at a time like this
the sky insistent, a helmet of gray
our children turning up mud
rocks in the side yard.
Layer after layer of tissue hearts
invade my panty drawer
try to speak for unbarred kisses
no nights of porn
your private emails.

It is February.
I have my thorns to bear.
The camellias splayed open
indecent in their anticipation of spring.
Last summer's lettuce gone
to muck in the back bed.
Fossilized longing.
The worm that eats the fruit in our heads.

Precision

The Northwest cloud banked
in love with itself, an oracle of rain
till my red shoes refuse to listen
sensible rubber wedged ones
take their place by the door.

In love with the weight of your voice
you tell me to buck up
act clever, efficient, accomplish things
pry the sky open.

I want to take your gold pocket watch
crush its precision
walk away with our two young children
the dog, cat, bicycles
smudge your attitude with a chalk stick

Come June the roses loosen their tongues
don't any longer need to beg for mercy
the sky remembers her blue trumpet
I roll down my thick stockings
latch a silver bracelet onto my ankle
watch the rufus red tail, hummingbirds flit
long for New England
a hammock stretched wide beside the river

knobby lives, poverty with its honest face
the lovemaking in other arms, other times
that might prosper.

There is a life each woman is heir to
sometimes complex, other times simple
woven of her own thread
the sun's unhampered testimony
a love of blue gentian
unfettered feet that press their
toes across rocky surfaces
marvel at the smooth tongue
of the wind's dimpling.

Sister

He brings midnight to your door
crushed rayon excuses
as if you are destined to be
only a paper thin wafer
cutout version in cinquefoil
chucking up cake batter
searching for god.

Midnight with its mudslides
drenched fire escape
his razors that shave close
pronounce a past clean.
There is purgatory on your plate
the facile smile that leaves once
the face finds itself a
less wanting companion.

Sister
no longer chic
no longer keeping the easy
premonition of roses
you eat the sun in your bed
the sickle of the moon the night raises
drown in jasmine
nakedness
the pulp of your body's wild fruit.

House Wife

You dabble in light
eat clouds, blue notebooks
gather the clipped moon
rain pawing
rinse sprouts, sieve cheese
water the sunflower greens
lift Lazarus

tend toasters, grilled cheese
bath time, runny noses
pray the light you send
will be durable geography
bend past midnight
and into a decent refrain.

Loyal friend
silent suitor
born of the almond tree
you spill honeysuckle across my table
crown my children gold
with the drizzle of your lamplight.

Weeds

In your eyes the world shoulders
hard working foot soldiers
minnows swimming against the stream.
I have seen you go off for days
with your heavy slung backpack
big boots
map of the North Cascades.

You are the hard bargainer
keeper of bird names, political treatises
topography maps
nail me to this house with your
sensible versions of paradise
acorn squash, spinach beds
endless watering.

My lover, you have blue eyes
a pearled face that can ambush
the fears of women
anger that is mostly a private affair
in bed bring durable hands, haste
hold a sturdy mind in a hungry age
wear your pants till the holes eat them.

This place grows weeds.
I leave them prostrate
room to feather the yard's skin.

White Slips

I want to believe decency
is more than the leaf mulch
that coats our yard's yielding
more than durable hands
the memory of my mother
coddling eggs, children
her lace, the empty clothesline.

Sometimes your hands are bullet proof
climb only pants pockets, car keys
are emissaries of spring's omission
the chromium field, secret emails.

On Sunday bands of peony, thistle
purple bells of the foxglove's leaning
flirt our yard.
I try to woo you on apricots
cashew cheese, chutney
my body's softest parable
many poems.

The girls in the white slips have risen early
slander the dawn with this other singing.

Reckoning

There is a place you come to
when the world stops needing you
becomes an empty page
devoid of hat spinning

like the first time you took me
ground down my derision
entered me

and ever since I've been spoken for
the vouchsafed homily
ink stained hands
periled breath
of how many snowstorms
bled out to sea.

Listen. I am nothing
in an arrested sea
only you are the juggernaut
the keen wind
the hand that guides
the hand upon this sail
the stars' reckoning.

Part Five

In the Bowl of Persimmons

Paradise

What if I didn't have my torn hankies
bits of torturous rope
and at last the day became itself
bird call, triple pink blossom of amaryllis
the rosemary scented indecent
sunflower seeds sprouting fitful
in the tray that claims sky

what would you make of my patchy
version of paradise, baggy dress
voice that choirs mossy syllables
disguised measures of content

would I wake up mysterious
or at least not bankrupt
no longer counting the day's lost sum
grammar lessons I failed to learn
content with my collapsed corridors
backyard colony of roses

would I meet you
round, flushed
rain smacked, muddy
an ambassador of light
exuberance that lifts roof tiles
plants a silver fork at your plate

what if there is no time
and the earth devours itself

before I can come nascent
what if I become a stranger
traitor, dilettante
dictator with too many hours missing
and the world turns arid uncensored
never comes to pronounce itself
amid summer's field burning

what if the moon finally swallows her tongue
the sun threatens to scorch us
then erase itself by diving into the sea

what if two and two no longer make four
and the color of reason turns out to be
a pretense to avoid marrying roses
and the suitcase you packed me
years ago, pigeon scented
is still a dispenser of broken wafer
lemon balm for the metal life I have forged
for that other part that never wanted
to go missing?

Small Voice

All night up on the fire escape
I try to conjure the stars
find the light hidden beneath
every house mantel
rabbits that refuse to be snatched.

It is no secret the moon
wants to be in many places
sets up no fixed foundation
only tents that move with the wind
joy amid the potholes.

The boy next door with the magnifying glass
lures the sun, scorches ants, grass
in the name of science
chalks the sidewalk with his regret.

You will become nothing in this life
my father used to tell me.
I was afraid of his hands, sadness
afraid of the sum of the world's aching
the grasshoppers someone will decide
to tear apart wing by wing.

Nightfall, you have no wired teeth.
I cleave to the fire escape
conjure the moon for my bed
this other lover

woo you on folktales, jasmine
colored thread.

Small voice
you are the tentative jarred seed
lapsed hour
elopement of how many young girls
in their unconquered blue dress
the lastness
of no name calling.

Lilacs

Paradise
there is no crown on your head
no early dismissal
from the day's mauling
only time with fugitive hands
the bill collector's retinol
my black lab whose life waits
on house keys, a red leash
the promise that dirt paths bring.

Promiscuous morning
paradise pronounces your name
under its breath
stealthy
almost imperceptible
as the lady slippers who slip their
sheerest negligees off for nothing
but the hands of the wind
the skunk cabbage mining the sun
of its yellow liquor
the farmhouse with its sloped porch
halted geraniums, rusted swing
how it once held the easy twined bodies
of new lovers in the grasp of its wing.

Paradise
you hide in the thistle
the busted clay pots
pump house with its spring fed well

in the arms of my children
once fractured by light
till this other world claims them.

I sit on my front steps
contemplate the waxwing's homily
the war zones we've cast
imagine my cursed hands
come back to life swollen as April
bunches of lavender whose lives
are all aroma and impending death.

On the back lawn
a tricycle leans on its side
rusting beside the blue tarp
my five and eight year old toss
their orange ball
ask what's for dinner
live only half impervious
to the vows we have set
to the silent ones
that get whittled away.

Come June

In the place we buried
the three gold fish
covered them in dirt
chipped beach shells
there has grown a calla lily
one single coronet
strikingly crimson
above sturdy leaves.

My two children look on.
I don't know how
to explain such things
the inauspicious gifts
the earth bestows.

Repentance

Cat, you gather the sun's kisses
sprawl your body out on the dirt
as if your life depends on it
this ease of lapping up heat.
Even our big black dog loosens
his anxious hold by my side
enters the yard's shapely.

Is this what I came for
the light's benevolence
hammock stretched across opposite poles
the body's limbering
loss of cramped shoes, clotheslines, dishes
the giving up of time
money with its big feet.

There are rope lines I want to enter freely
my bare feet fluid as a woman
in love with the shape of the earth
guileless, saucy in her summer dress
reverent for the sake of the world's breaking
cognizant that *your* song is everything
no one left hungry
on this day in that world.

Today green bread for the taking.
The dog, the cat eat up
uncivilized creatures that they are.
The net cast out between two poles.

The thyme, rosemary bushes
finding their way back
the myrtle busting forth beside the sand turtle
shovels, camellia petals floating in buckets
the children's projects sprawled across the yard.
Come back to me then.
For I have inked leaves on my tongue
a mysterious kingdom
uneasy devotion to home.

Restitution

Blinded eye
you track the sun's exuberance
stumble down wharfs
harbor seals, the dead kitten
last season's pansies
the toy soldier with a split seam.

Some say blindness
becomes its own sort of dictionary
nails the memory of glass bulbed Christmas
permanently inside the head
scurries past minefields
drowns us in the scent of mint, lavender
smell of bacon frying
thick coffee.

Some say that the soul grows wings.
You open your mouth around
the ruby nocturne of peaches
genuflect for safe crossing the road
know every stranger's hand
could be the one that leads home
do not envy
what you cannot see
and in not seeing
restitute the world beautiful.

Blinded eye
you blend with the scenery
gather convulsed sunset

the lost prayer book
chalk games of children
anchor with a stilled gaze
consume the harder nighttime
of our divided days
as if longing is a child's blank slate
god leaking
into our empty pocket.

Street Woman

You dangle the cross
mind the street sweepers homilies
voices of children
whose feet lift buoyant

hum your blue resolve
into the day
thin boned
no drunken retinol
of the sky's bleeding

wear a bud embossed dress
with its summer tongue
singing

walk on tightrope
the invisible
god's inebriation.

God

You who hold the earth's greening
shape pig, cow, chicken, chestnuts
soothe the stranger on the hill
you who create octopus, starfish
the cloud's smoky allegiance
the old couple loving each other
senseless inside the rain
we thank you

the child who swallowed midnight
drank from your well
the boy with the limp leg
misshapen dog
woman bowed down with cancer
all cleave to more than your name

you are the cup, the root
the ruby wine, inaugural morning
the lamplight's faithful

ages pass, cities rise up, slope away
civilizations tack nails to their wings
ground themselves
others become weightless
fly from the world's weeping

you are spindrift
the dreamer's pillow

moon's lip service
shy voice of jasmine

stay close then
for heaven is a whisper
palm of dust
blue flower's flame
the filigree of so many petals
your hand casts out
to float or die
in the wind.

You Collude with the Wind

wage war on pestilence
anchor stellar jays to my tree
calm the man plagued by scissors
the mercenary yard
city's restless
death with its hand grenades
barbed feet.

When the cawing of the day
brings its nine invisible blades
that auger the heart
you are the weathered stone
rubbed smooth by lament
the pockmarked face
ruby sheep pawing

you are the trials of winter
boy with the rock laced snowball
old woman whose life is a memory of poems
the lastness of the stone's singing.

I have seen you wrestle truculent angels
lovers with glass in their bed
unbend hope
perk up the limp stem of roses
till they find a secret fountain.

Stillness may never claim me
rinse all the brine

obliterate the wounds that have festered.
But let me be the crystal that rings
as she's breaking
an animal whose clear eyed devotion
bolsters the blue heart

in the realm of sorrow
let me be the last note
that enters the torn page
the basket of eggs
bread's leavening
in the mouths of children
become sustenance
song.

In the Bowl of Persimmons

I see the consecration of your hands
weight of them
remember this angular walk
toward darkness
we consume in our beds
the voracity of your twin mountain streams
perfect pawing.

In the bowl of persimmons
I feel the elliptical nature of paradise
the inauguration of sparrows
twining their twig nests in the tree
the round stones that border
the garden's fruitful
the map home for the lost man.

I sense the weight of your allegiance
love's quiet threads
you by the farmhouse in scant clothing
reciting the elegies of Rilke under the stars
inside the field's secret burning.

In the bowl of persimmons
I taste the pulp and pith
of our lives here
the strength of your hands
hoisting my waist through the hiatus
of shade trees

the treacherous disposition of roses
worship that stumbles through madness
broken bread.

Drown me then.
For already I have spoken more
than we mortals may dare.
You are the cup, the hands
the fruit, the bowl, the waking
my body's refuge
and revenge
this paradise I hold in my bed.

Epilogue

Who would care if
one day the angel of God
came down and devoured me
and I am left shoeless
all my nights failing
your one last word wedged
like a parapet upon my lips

as if in your savioring
I am set free
almost jubilant
among the withered things
the trees aching

this other table
you have set
for me.

Toni Thomas lives in Portland, Oregon. Her poems have been published in Austria, Spain, New Zealand, Canada, England, Scotland, and Australia. In the United States her work has appeared in over fifty literary magazines including
Prairie Schooner, North Dakota Quarterly,
Hayden's Ferry Review, the Minnesota Review,
Notre Dame Review, Poetry East, and more. She has been twice nominated for a Pushcart prize, and won several awards. She has published twenty-five collections of poetry and six books for children.

Her figurative clay sculptures have been shown in gallery exhibits in Portland and Chicago, displayed in literary magazines, and housed in private collections in the U.S. and England.

Her short documentary *One of Us* was shown at the Trans-ideology: Nostalgia festival in Berlin and at the Museum of Contemporary Art in Taipei.

Since Toni loves to create and sits buried in reams of poems, manuscripts, clay figures and images....she likes to imagine all of them out in the world swaying wild as the lupine.

tonithomaspoetry.com

www.ingramcontent.com/pod-product-compliance
Lightning Source LLC
Chambersburg PA
CBHW030454010526
44118CB00011B/938